FORTUNE COOKIES

FORTUNE COOKIES

*Management Wit and Wisdom
from <u>FORTUNE</u> Magazine*

Edited by Alan Deutschman
Conceived by Leslie Gaines-Ross

VINTAGE BOOKS
A DIVISION OF RANDOM HOUSE, INC.
NEW YORK

A VINTAGE ORIGINAL, FIRST EDITION, MAY 1993

Copyright © 1987, 1988, 1989, 1990, 1991, 1992, 1993 by Time, Inc.

All rights reserved under International and Pan-American Copyright Conventions. Published in the United States by Vintage Books, a division of Random House, Inc., New York, and simultaneously in Canada by Random House of Canada Limited, Toronto.

The contents of this work were previously published in FORTUNE magazine in 1987–1993.

Library of Congress Cataloging-in-Publication Data
Fortune cookies: management wit and wisdom from FORTUNE magazine / edited by Alan Deutschman.   p. cm.
ISBN 0-679-74592-0
1. Quotations, English.   2. Business—Quotations, maxims, etc.
3. Management—maxims, etc.   I. Deutschman, Alan, 1965–
II. Fortune.
PN6084.B87F67   1993
650—dc20   92-50705
CIP

BOOK DESIGN BY JO BONNEY

Books are available at special discounts for bulk purchases (100 copies or more) for sales promotions or premiums. For more information, call Special Marketing, 1-800-800-3246.

Manufactured in the United States of America

10 9 8 7 6 5 4 3 2

CONTENTS

In the fifth century B.C., a heathen came to the famed Rabbi Hillel and said he would convert to Judaism if the rabbi could teach him the entire Torah "while standing on one foot." Hillel replied, "What is hateful to you, do not unto your neighbor. This is the entire Torah, all the rest is commentary." One of the great thinkers of our own time, the late physicist Richard Feynman, opened his lecture course for Cal Tech freshmen by asking, "If in some cataclysm all of scientific knowledge were to be destroyed and only one sentence passed on to the next generation of creatures, what statement would contain the most information in the fewest words?"

The statements in this book were chosen because they convey the most information about the manager's world—leadership, customer service, sales and marketing, quality, innovation, strategy, among other topics—in the fewest words. We hope they in turn will inspire further thought on the part of readers.

We trust you'll find these sayings useful and insightful. In a pinch, you could even read them while standing on one foot—or while waiting for a commuter train or a connecting flight. As the motto reads on the notebook of Warnaco CEO Linda Wachner: DO IT NOW!

—Alan Deutschman

FORTUNE COOKIES

VISION

In most organizations, the future doesn't have a lobbying group.

"Visionary leadership rather than managerial skill will be the most valued standard for tomorrow's top officer."

—Lester Korn,
co-founder of the Korn-Ferry
executive search firm

◆

The visionary must be able to communicate what he has dreamed, and his company must have the panoply of technical skills needed to execute it.

What makes a vision inspiring?

1. *A challenge so big or audacious that it can seem scary even to the person who conceived it.*

2. *Some purpose higher than the everyday getting and spending of commerce.*

Lay out a very broad vision and then let divisions develop their own business strategies. Let employees know that there is no rigid master plan.

LEADERSHIP

Communication is the most important source of personal power.

◆

Don't underestimate the power symbolic gestures have on workers.

"Lech Walesa told Congress that there is a declining market for words. He's right. The only thing the world believes is behavior, because they see it instantaneously. None of us may preach anymore. We must behave."

—Max DePree,
chairman of Herman Miller

An experienced operating manager, given the right guidance, can almost invariably do a better job than someone from corporate headquarters.

◆

"We have to undo a 100-year-old concept and convince our managers that their role is not to control people and stay 'on top' of things, but rather to guide, energize, and excite."

—Jack Welch,
CEO of General Electric

"You can't control people, especially Americans, but you can enlist their support."

—Rollie Boreham,
CEO of Baldor Electric

You don't have to make everyone walk in lockstep if you're sure each one is heading in the right direction.

Manage in response to the consumer market, not the stock market.

◆

The sale is a courtship. How good the marriage is depends on how well the seller maintains the relationship.

◆

Never criticize a staffer for making a customer happy.

Think of yourself as the customer. Identify with your clientele.

♦

Workers who treat one another well serve customers better.

♦

The more closely a company's work force mirrors its customer base, the more effectively it will be able to design and sell its products.

Think of every product you buy or sell as a service. In other words, look at what it does, not what it is. That way, selling a product becomes only one of your opportunities to do something for your customer.

◆

Today's buyers know what they want and how much they're willing to pay.

Southwest Airlines insists on capitalizing the word *customer* wherever it is used—in ads, brochures, even the annual report. The practice may seem picayune, but what better way to flag employees and the public that the Customer matters?

"If we listened to market research about our traditional customers, we would go out of business. . . . Look for customers who aren't satisfied . . . and demand what we aren't doing today."

—Ed McCracken,
CEO of Silicon Graphics

When every customer demands special service, every sales rep has to have the power to offer it.

◆

The best—and cheapest—way to keep customers satisfied is to serve them well from the start.

Listen to customers. They're quite willing to say what kind of service they want and to rate the service they're getting.

◆

Eliminate the bureaucracy that often makes it difficult for customers to register complaints or render suggestions.

Customers tell twice as many people about bad
experiences as good ones.

♦

"Turning away a complainer by telling him, 'It's our
policy,' enrages him. That's the corporate equivalent
of your parents saying, 'Because I said so.'"
            —Richard Whitely,
                president, Forum Corporation

When companies make their customers happy, they make their employees happy too. Improvements in customer satisfaction lead directly to higher employee retention.

◆

"Customers are first, employees second, shareholders third, and the community fourth." That's the credo at H. B. Fuller, the century-old adhesives maker in St. Paul.

SALES AND MARKETING

"What you really need in a service business is people who like people."
> —Frank Petro,
> consultant, Booz · Allen & Hamilton

◆

The successful sales rep of this decade will be a facilitator, not a pitchman, an expert on the customer's total business who coordinates with colleagues to make buying easy and efficient.

◆

Listen to everyone who helps get goods to market.

Don't let advertising hype create consumer expectations that rise faster than service can improve.

♦

Use toll-free lines and comment cards only to supplement incessant customer surveys.

Americans no longer trust manufacturers. Consumers are bombarded with information that conflicts with what the companies are saying.

♦

"Every company should have an environmental team that is directly linked to the CEO and the board."
—Anita Roddick,
founder of Body Shop International

"The growing appetite for products will come from the Third World, and its ambitions and demands will mimic in most ways everything that has gone before in Western society. Once television is there, people of whatever shade, culture, or origin want roughly the same things."

—Anthony O'Reilly,
CEO of H. J. Heinz

Superachieving service companies are imbued with the belief that profits come from providing genuine value.

◆

"In [consumer] research, averages are going to mean nothing. If you're looking for 20 percent of the people who are crazy about it and can't live without it, and if 80 percent hate it, so what?"

—Laurel Cutler,
vice-chairman of FCB/Leber
Katz advertising agency

"It's easy to make a videotape about the company's strategy and vision. What's tough is to make sure they're showing the tapes in the plant in Turkey."

—Reuben Mark,
CEO of Colgate-Palmolive

Use technology to give your workers the information they need to serve the customer and the time to attend to him.

◆

Accept the reality that technology can best be used to support workers, not replace them.

QUALITY

"The value decade is upon us. If you can't sell a top-quality product at the world's lowest price, you're going to be out of the game."

—Jack Welch

♦

Quality can and should be affordable. The dramatic improvement in the quality of most products over the past decade or so helped create the new psychology of value. As manufacturers everywhere have improved goods, buyers' expectations have soared. The Japanese call this *atarimae hinshitsu*, which means "quality taken for granted."

Practice "rapid inch-up": take enough tiny steps and pretty soon you outdistance the competition.

◆

Give workers defined targets to hit and get them involved in their jobs.

To improve manufacturing quality, use teams of workers cross-trained in several skills. They can detect flaws in each other's work, apply problem-solving techniques, and fill in for each other as needed.

◆

Shift responsibility for detecting defects from inspectors at the end of the assembly line to individual production workers.

To invent products out of thin air, you don't ask people what they want—you ask them what problems they have when they get up in the morning. Who would have told you ten years ago that they needed a CD player?

TEN COMMANDMENTS OF QUALITY

1. *Quality can always get better.*

2. *Quality is everybody's business.*

3. *Some of the best ideas will come from the most unexpected sources.*

4. *Talking about quality isn't enough—develop a detailed implementation plan.*

5. *The departmental, territorial imperative is quality's biggest obstacle.*

6. *Set quality standards for each step in each job.*

7. *You must know why and when something goes wrong.*

8. *Be patient: don't expect gains in the next quarter.*

9. *Make extraordinary efforts in unusual situations. Customers will remember those best.*

10. *Think beyond cutting costs. The benefits of improved quality should reach every part of the organization.*

INNOVATION

Innovate or evaporate.

♦

Let it be known that risk takers won't be penalized
for new ideas that fail.

Make clear to one and all that the future of the enterprise rests on a willingness to experiment, to push in new and untested directions.

◆

"You can't win by comparing yourself to where you were last year. You've got to remember that the other guy is learning, too, so you actually have to go faster than the leader to catch up."
—Ralph Gomory,
president of Alfred P. Sloan Foundation

Avoid spending too much time and money on "trombone oil projects": you may turn out the best product in the world, but the entire world needs only about a pint of the stuff each year.

"The key to success . . . in business, science, and technology . . . is never to follow the others."

♦

"I never had much use for specialists. Specialists are inclined to argue why you can't do something, while our emphasis has always been to make something out of nothing."

—Masaru Ibuka,
founder of Sony

"Hire people of youth and vitality, people who are chronic grumblers about the status quo."
>—Warren Bennis,
>professor of management,
>University of Southern California

Get out of the office and talk to people on the shop floor and in the most far-flung outposts of your corporate empire.

♦

Emphasize that each employee should develop several competencies.

Put those nice new MBAs—even the ones from Harvard—on the manufacturing line for more than a ceremonial visit so they understand the difficulty of the factory environment and have respect for the people out there.

"Management development planning must be elevated to a priority at least equal to that of the corporate acquisitions team and other profit-generating operations."

—Lester Korn

Help workers learn by urging them to visit other factories, trade shows, customers, and, if possible, the competition.

◆

Don't underestimate the power of bigger bucks to attract higher-quality workers and improve service.

"Companies simply can't prosper in a diverse, multicultural world unless they reflect that diversity to some degree."

—James Houghton,
CEO of Corning

"We promote people quickly, out of a fear that our best people will be swiped if we don't."

—Roy Vagelos,
CEO of Merck

JACK WELCH'S SIX RULES

1. *Face reality as it is, not as it was or as you wish it to be.*

2. *Be candid with everyone.*

3. *Don't manage, lead.*

4. *Change before you have to.*

5. *If you don't have a competitive advantage, don't compete.*

6. *Control your own destiny, or someone else will.*

Be willing to accept years of losses to create a new market.

◆

Whether it's broke or not, fix it—make it better—not just products, but the whole company if necessary.

In industries filled with entrenched giants, newcomers have a big advantage: they draw on a clean slate.

"We've got to create a 'boundaryless' company. We no longer have the time to climb over barriers between functions like engineering and marketing, or between people—hourly, salaried, management, and the like."

—Jack Welch

♦

Saying "we have such a large market share" is no excuse for complacency—there are companies that are market leaders and still earn a little bit larger share year after year.

Show an unqualified willingness to accept a variety of opinions and integrate them into your management style.

◆

"My style is to encourage controversy and encourage people to say what they think."
—James Burke,
former CEO of Johnson & Johnson

Delegate real responsibility to subordinates.

◆

A boss genuinely interested in what his people have
to say will not state his own opinions first.

"Twenty-first-century managers cannot simply be masters of the balance sheet."

—Lester Korn

Keep your personal staff to a minimum.
Chamberlains and gatekeepers almost always end up
filtering information.

♦

Make sure that the group of people who report to
you directly includes at least a few independent
minds. You may have to tolerate considerable
eccentricity and not a little unhappiness among the
rest of the troops.

Be exquisitely careful how you receive less-than-glad tidings. No tirades, no tight-lipped sarcasm, no pushing back the table, no eyes rolling upward. Ask calm, even-tempered questions.

◆

Establish regular times when people know they can come and see you. Better yet, go to their offices to talk to them.

The biggest mistakes that managers make in hiring is choosing only those who look as if they would fit in.

Give employees information. They can't feel in control of circumstances if they lack it.

◆

The least stressed employees are those who are working flat out on some task that *they* have selected—something they really love to do.

Managers should set realistic deadlines and go out of their way not to change them.

◆

A manager should work on his capacity to embrace the novel and unexpected.

"A 'Copernican revolution' must take place in the attitudes of American CEOs as the international economy no longer revolves around the U.S. and the world market is shared by many strong players."
—Lester Korn

♦

Replace profit centers based on countries or regions with ones based on product lines.

♦

In markets that you cannot penetrate on your own, find allies.

"Glocalize," as the Japanese call it: make global decisions on strategic questions about products, capital, and research, but let local units decide tactical questions about packaging, marketing, and advertising.

COMMUNICATION

"What you tell the outside world has to be the same
thing you tell your senior people, and the same thing
you tell your factory workers."

—Reuben Mark

◆

Explain things—personally. Communicating with
employees has a positive impact on job satisfaction.

◆

If you don't now survey employee attitudes, start.
What you find can help identify problems before
they become crises.

Play it straight with employees and don't withhold bad news until the last minute. Give as much advance warning as possible.

◆

Make sure your door is really open. CEOs can't recall employees ever abusing an open-door policy: they don't walk through it unless they really have to.

Body Shop invites workers to make suggestions on bathroom walls—and gets the occasional "gem of an idea," says founder Anita Roddick.

The most enlightening employee polls are those that ask the toughest questions.

Make the CEO responsible for press relations. He or she must often speak for the corporation, routinely and in times of crisis.

◆

Release the bad news yourself—before some reporter digs it up.

If you screw up, admit it candidly. Avoid hedging or excuses. Apologize, promise not to do it again, and explain how you're going to make things right.

♦

Tell the truth—or nothing. Nobody likes a liar.

MORALE

To achieve real empowerment and improve morale, follow three basic steps:

1. *Find out what people are thinking, what they believe the problems in the company are.*

2. *Let them design the solutions.*

3. *Get out of the way and let them put those solutions into practice.*

The key to making a high-commitment organization work is mutual trust between top executives and employees.

Companies can provide big-time relief for parents with small gestures: making a telephone available to assembly-line workers so they can check up on their latchkey kids, say, or letting office workers slip out for a parent-teacher conference without a hassle.

◆

Professionals who have flexible work schedules are fiercely loyal to their employers. Grateful for the treatment they have received, they strive to prove themselves worthy of the company's trust.

Don't disdain the hokey. On Thanksgiving, Gulfstream CEO Allen Paulson dons a chef's hat and serves turkey to his employees, wishing each one well by name. On Valentine's Day, Southwest Airlines CEO Herb Kelleher sends out 8,200 personalized valentines.

Change from lean and mean to lean and *not* mean. Of all the factors contributing to burnout, job uncertainty tops the list—workers terrified of getting the ax are most likely to push themselves too far or just give up and quit trying.

◆

Sometimes burnout prevention can be as simple as making sure managers take their vacations each year or occasionally giving them a surprise three-day weekend.

The four-to-one rule: For every criticism you make of a worker's performance, give him or her four compliments.

Tie the financial interests of the higher-ups and lower-downs closer together by making exposure to risk and reward more equitable.

◆

Make sure that incentive compensation is linked to performance over which the beneficiaries have control.

Work on being approachable. Avoid imperial trappings—the cavernous office, the executive dining room, the dark-windowed limo.

♦

"If you don't treat your own people well, they won't treat other people well."

—Herb Kelleher,
CEO of Southwest Airlines

TARGETING CHANGE

Realize that the race is often won by those who get a new idea to market fastest and best rather than by those who create it.

◆

The worst way to speed up a company is by trying to make it do things just as it does, only faster. The machinery—and certainly the workers—will simply burn out. Instead, start from scratch.

◆

Take a hard look at the number of times a product or service requires some sort of approval before reaching the customer.

Most people don't know how their own company works. Make a flow chart of your administrative processes to show workers what's really happening.

◆

"In Japan we set a clear size and ease-of-use target for a consumer or business product from the very beginning. The target comes first, often before we have the technology to achieve it. That's why we move faster."

—Masaru Ibuka

Six things an executive should never delegate:

1. *planning*

2. *selecting the team*

3. *monitoring their efforts*

4. *motivating*

5. *evaluating*

6. *rewarding.*

Edited from FORTUNE's *interview with Miss Manners (Judith Martin):*

"If you're in the same meeting and your boss says something factually wrong, do not contradict your boss in public. If the information is trivial, let it pass. If it's essential, find a tactful way of bringing the material in without contradicting him."

◆

"Don't feel obligated to raise a question or make a comment in a meeting. If you don't have anything worthwhile to contribute, shut up."

"If someone lays claim to your work in a meeting, you
should speak up. Business matters don't require you
to be self-effacing."

◆

"If you're playing tennis with the boss, you don't
have to let him win. Etiquette does not require you
to falsify your achievements in any respect in order
to ingratiate yourself with people."

◆

"You should not invite your boss to dinner. Absolutely
not. You should instead put your energy into
impressing him with what a good job you can do."

Resist cutbacks. In a recession, consider some of the alternatives to layoffs: curb new hiring, pare contingent workers, use voluntary leaves, reduce pay, share the work, or encourage early retirement.

◆

"If you're strong, look at recession as an opportunity to deliver the death blow to some marginal players."
—Edward Lawler III,
professor of management,
University of Southern California

During recessions the last thing you want to do is skimp on customer service, even though this might mean forgoing some cost savings. When Delta Air Lines tried to save money by serving pretzels instead of peanuts, customers hated it.

◆

Customers are more fickle than ever in hard times. They are not going to wait around while you, for cost reasons, keep your new products on hold, especially when the competition develops theirs.

At a time when most companies are obsessed with nipping and tucking costs, bold ones look for ways to grow by spending on advertising, new products, and acquisitions.

◆

Candor can be especially crucial when a company faces tough times.

Peter Drucker argues for companies to set aside 10 percent to 12 percent of annual expenditures for R&D, employee development, and other investments in growth—in bad times as well as good.

Boldness may well be the preeminent competitive advantage in this slow-growth decade. When the herd merely tinkers while waiting for demand to pick up, smart companies are engaged in organizational revolution, altering radically how work is done.

Warnaco CEO Linda Wachner carries a well-worn spiral notebook with the words DO IT NOW embossed on the cover in big black letters.

♦

"No one ever lost a sale by listening too closely."
—Robert Epstein,
co-founder of Sybase

FOR FURTHER READING

These "cookies" were excerpted from numerous issues of FORTUNE
that appeared from 1987 to 1993. For readers interested in delving further
into particular topics, the following articles should prove helpful.
(For reprints of any article,
write to FORTUNE, Time & Life Building, Room 1537,
Rockefeller Center, New York, N.Y. 10020.)

VISION
"A Hard Look at Executive Vision," October 23, 1989.

LEADERSHIP
"The Seven Keys to Business Leadership," October 24, 1988.

CUSTOMER SERVICE
"How to Deal with Tougher Customers," December 3, 1990;
"What Customers Really Want," June 4, 1990;
"Getting Customers to Love You," March 13, 1989;
"How to Handle Customers' Gripes," October 24, 1988.

SALES AND MARKETING
"How to Remake Your Sales Force," May 4, 1992.

THE TEN COMMANDMENTS OF QUALITY
"Victories in the Quality Crusade," October 10, 1988.
"How to Prosper in the Value Decade," November 30, 1992

INNOVATION
"America's Fastest-Growing Companies," October 5, 1992;

"How Sony Keeps the Magic Going," February 24, 1992;
"The Innovation Gap," December 2, 1991.

PEOPLE/COMMUNICATION/MORALE

"The Morale Crisis," November 18, 1991;
"The Trust Gap," December 4, 1989.

JACK WELCH'S SIX RULES

"Inside the Mind of Jack Welch," March 27, 1989.

THE ART OF MANAGING

"How to Escape the Echo Chamber," June 18, 1990.

GOING GLOBAL

"How to Go Global—And Why," August 28, 1989.

SPEED

"How Managers Can Succeed Through Speed," February 13, 1989.

HARD TIMES

"How to Thrive in a Lame Economy," October 5, 1992;
"How to Manage in a Recession," November 5, 1990.

CEO PERSPECTIVES

"What I Want U.S. Business to Do in '92," December 30, 1991;
The New American Century, special issue, Spring/Summer 1991;
"Today's Leaders Look to Tomorrow," March 26, 1990.

In loving memory of Ben Arnold

Special thanks to Tom Kulaga, sales promotion director
at FORTUNE, whose imagination and support carried this
book into being; to Virginia Green and George Krauter, for
the original cover design; to Walter Kiechel III, for
encouragement and guidance; and to the fine stewardship of
Marshall Loeb, FORTUNE's managing editor, for yielding
so many splendid FORTUNE Cookies from which
to choose.

And for our editor, Marty Asher, we offer our very own
FORTUNE Cookie: "Think small—reap big rewards."

—Leslie Gaines-Ross
Marketing Director, FORTUNE
April 1993

"Be realistic—demand the impossible."

—*sign in the office of T. J. Rodgers,*
founder and CEO of Cypress Semiconductor